# smell

First U.S. edition published 1985 by Barron's Educational Series, Inc.

© Parramón Ediciones, S.A., 1983

All inquiries should be addressed to:
Barron's Educational Series, Inc.
250 Wireless Boulevard
Hauppauge, New York 11788

International Standard Book No. 0-8120-3565-8

Library of Congress Catalog Card No. 84-28209

**Library of Congress Cataloging in Publication Data**

Parramón, José María
  The fives senses—smell.

  Translation of: Los cinco sentidos—el olfato.
  Summary: A short scientific explanation of our sense
of smell, with a diagram of the nose.
  1. Smell—Juvenile literature. [1. Smell.  2. Nose.
3. Senses and sensation]  I. Puig, J.J.  II. Rius, María, ill.
III. Title.
QP458.P3613    1985      612'.86      84-28209
ISBN 0-8120-3565-8

0 1 2 3    0 9 8

Register Book Number: 785
Legal Deposit: B-6723-90

Printed in Spain by Emsa
Diputación, 116 - 08015 Barcelona

# the five senses

# smell

## María Rius
## J.M. Parramón   J.J. Puig

CHILDRENS PRESS CHOICE

A Barron's title selected for educational distribution

ISBN 0-516-08688-X

Smell the flowers…

...and the cake, fresh from the oven!

Smell the cows in the barn.

Smell Mommy's perfume…

...the salty breezes when you're way out to sea...

...and the lavender in the meadow.

Smell the wood burning
in a campfire.

Smell the fish that were just caught...

...the bread that was just baked...

...and the damp earth after rain.

How good it is to smell hot soup!

Everything that you smell, you smell with your NOSE.

# SMELL

Your *nose* is much simpler than your other sense organs. Your eyes, your ears, and your skin have many more different parts, and different jobs. But your sense of smell is very important to you. Not only does it let you know what smells good and what doesn't, but your sense of smell also helps you taste the food that you eat. Actually, a large part of your sense of taste is really your nose sending your brain messages about smell at the same time.

If you have a cold, and your nose is all stuffed up, you'll find that whatever you eat has hardly any taste at all.

Here is how your nose works. When dinner is cooking in the kitchen, tiny little particles of the food, which are too small for you to see, are floating through the air. These little pieces of food get carried up into your nose. There, the *olfactory nerve* carries the message to your brain about what's for dinner.

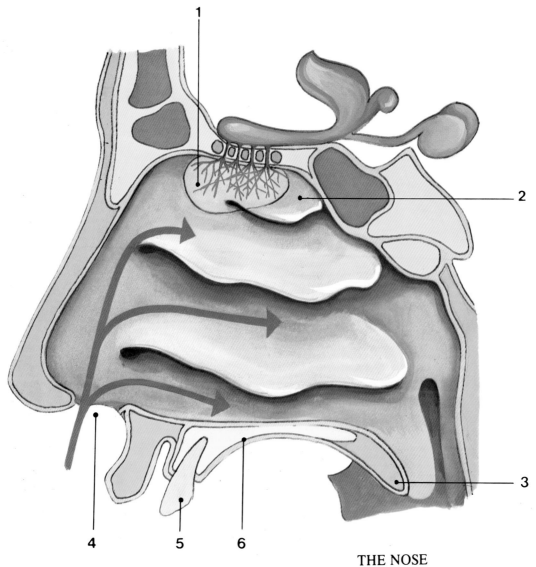

## THE NOSE

1  Olfactory nerve
2  Sinus
3  Palate
4  Nostril
5  Teeth
6  Roof of your mouth

# SMELL

The olfactory nerves are located very high up in your nasal passage. That's why you don't always smell an odor right away. Sometimes it takes a while for the tiny particles to get all the way up to the thousands of little nerve endings.

Human beings have a very weak sense of smell. As people evolved, they didn't need to smell things quite as well as other animals did. They could use their eyes and their brains in a different way.

Dogs, for example, have a very highly developed sense of smell. They can smell things the same way humans see colors and understand language. A dog can smell his master coming home, even before he can see him. A dog can also smell where his master has been, what he had for lunch, or whether he sat next to someone who owned a cat. That's a lot of information to get from smell alone, isn't it?

Some people develop their sense of smell for a particular use. A perfume maker can tell all the different flowers from each other by their different smells. A wine maker has the same talent for telling different wines from each other by their smell.

There is another way that your sense of smell is different from all your other senses. After a while, your sense of smell gets tired. When you first come into the house, you can smell dinner cooking, but after that your olfactory nerves get overtired. Then you don't smell anything at all.

Smell is one of the ways you have of knowing about your world. Close your eyes and smell a rose, or after a long winter, go outside. That nice green smell tells you spring is here.